Bubba the Coughing Bee (Otherwise Known as the Bee Who Had a Very Bad Cold) by Matthew Badeaux

Published by
HigherLife Publishing & Marketing, Inc.
PO Box 623307
Oviedo, FL 32762
www.ahigherlife.com

ISBN: 978-0-9994156-8-9
ebook ISBN: 978-1-939183-89-7

Illustrated by: Lisa Mikler

First Edition
16 17 18 19 20 21 — 9 8 7 6 5 4 3 2 1
Printed in the United States of America

# Bubba the Coughing Bee

## (Otherwise Known as the Bee Who Had a Very Bad Cold)

By Matthew Badeaux

Illustrated by Lisa Mikler

eep in the woods, high up on a sycamore tree, was a beehive. And inside the beehive you could hear a very loud yell:

"Bubba! If I told you once, I told you a thousand times, you've got to eat your honey, honey, or you're gonna catch a cold! Now, you get your little bee-hind to your bedroom and wait 'til your father gets back to the hive! Boy, is he gonna give you a stingin' you ain't never gonna forget!"

"Yes, Mama. I'm sorry, Mama," sobbed Bubba.

So, Bubba went to his bedroom feeling quite low in spirits and thinking to himself that it was bad enough getting yelled at by his mama, now he had to wait for his papa to come home and get a stingin'. Everyone knows how painful that could be! And that's when Bubba decided it was time to fly the hive. But before he flew, he left a note. And it read something like this...

deer moma and poppa

i hav desided to fli away frum the hive cuzz i have a very bad coled an i didint want to git a stingen frum poppa. i'm not comming bak til i fine a crue for mi coff an mi coled.

luv bubba

pea ess poppa? r yu stil gonna sting mee if i com bak?

As Bubba finished his letter, he rested his tired bee head on his desk, perhaps gathering up strength for his journey. He then sighed, "I just wanted to fly around with my friends. I didn't really think I'd get yelled at by Mama just for getting a cold...And now I'm getting a stingin' from Papa."

Bubba then closed his eyes for just a moment and thought, "I wonder where I could find a cure for my cold? Hmm…Where?"

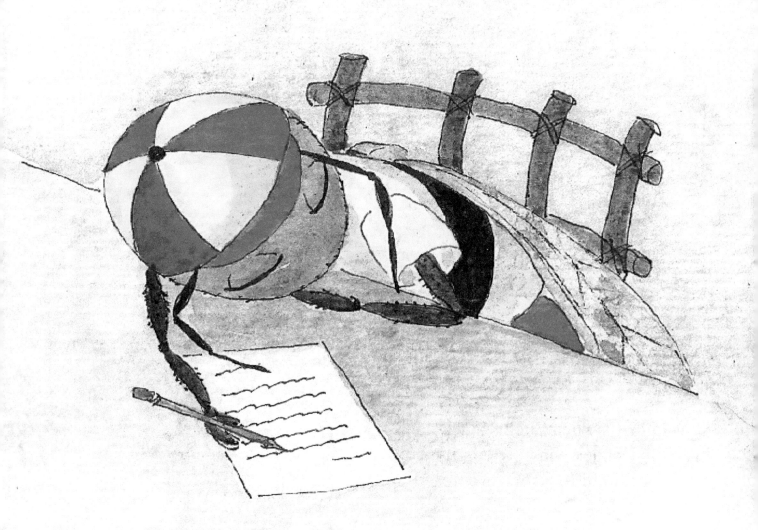

And that's when Bubba snuck behind his mama's back and flew out of the hive to begin his quest for a cure.

As Bubba flew over a herd of cows and just passed old Farmer John's pond, a sinking feeling overtook him a brief moment, for he had never flown so far from his hive.

But then, he saw a red-brown fox who appeared to be hunting for something crouched low behind a bush. Bubba decided to get a closer look at the fox when a sudden gust of wind blew his little bee-hind right smack in front of the fox's face.

"Hey! Buzz off, bee! You're wrecking my concentration on my lunch over there! Get outta here!" yelled the fox.

"Sorry about that, Mr. Fox, but my name's Bubba and I've got this cold. And I thought maybe you might know of a cure. You see, I don't want to go back to the beehive and get a stingin' from my papa. So, do you think you could help me find a cure? Huh, Mr. Fox?" asked Bubba, as he coughed and fluttered his wings.

"Shhh!" hushed the fox in his best angry whisper. "Keep your wings down! You're gonna scare away my lunch! Man! Isn't it enough youse guys got them there stingers? Let alone a little bee with a cough! Who ever heard of such a thing? Wait'll I tell the guys at the fox hole…A coughing bee!" mocked the fox.

Bubba looked at the fox and was tempted to fly over to his nose and give him a good stingin'. But all bees know that a stingin' should only be applied as a last resort. Besides, Bubba needed answers, not enemies.

"Now you listen to me, Bubba!" said the Fox. "I haven't had a meal since I got out of a beaver trap two days ago. And if you scare away my lunch, I'm gonna have a sudden change on my menu and put you on it! You get the point? Understand, Bubba?" snarled the fox, who was probably more hungry than angry.

"Oh, I won't scare away your lunch, Mr. Fox."

"Don't call me Mr. Fox!" interrupted the now very hungry fox. "The name's Sticky Paws. And that's not because I've got honey on them, Bubba. Listen!"

"I don't know nothin' about no cure for no cough, especially for no bee! Why don't you just go ask the Great White Owl? He knows everything. Just buzz off and leave me alone! My stomach's growling!" complained Sticky Paws.

"The Great White Owl, huh? Mr. Fox—I mean Stinky Paws without the honey? How do I find the Great White Owl? Huh? Where does he live?" asked Bubba.

As Bubba waited for an answer, he noticed the eyes of Sticky Paws were completely focused on his "lunch." But the hungry fox managed to whisper a few angry words to Bubba as he fixed his eyes on his prey.

"Ah! Well...he lives somewhere in the forest. Would you leave me alone, now? I don't wanna catch your cold. You shouldn't be lookin' for owls anyway. Where I come from you don't go lookin' for trouble. Trouble finds you. And besides, I'm just about ready to make my move. We foxes are expert hunters, ya see? So, I've gotta concentrate. Understand?"

"Thank you, Stinky Paws without the honey. The forest, huh? By the way, what are you trying to catch for lunch?" asked Bubba, not really wanting to know, but trying to be polite.

"You see that mouse over there, on top

of that tree stump?" whispered Sticky Paws.

"You mean the one that just ran away? I see it, Mr. Stinky Paws."

"Oh, I hate that when that happens! Look what you did! Can't a hungry fox eat a little fast food, here, without a sick little bee with a cold scaring it away?" growled Sticky Paws.

"I'm sorry about your lunch, Mr. Stinky Paws without the honey. Thanks for telling me about the Great White Owl, though. Bye!" shouted Bubba who speedily flew away from the growling fox.

"Grrrh! The name's STICKY Paws! STICKY... Not Stinky! Sticky!"

As Bubba flew away from the growling Sticky Paws without the honey, who lost his lunch, he made his way toward the forest in search of the Great White Owl. Lo and behold, just below him on the ground, he could see Sticky Paws' ex-lunch skittering toward the forest and heading to the safety behind a rock.

Bubba then thought to himself: "Surely a mouse would know where owls live." So he decided to buzz on down and have a little chat with the little rat...ahh...mouse.

"Man! That was a close one, man!" huffed the mouse. "I almost became taco meat for El Fox over there. I'll chew his face off! Nobody messes with El Chico Mouse. Oh, I'll chew his face off with my teeth!" yelled El Chico Mouse. At this moment Bubba was attempting to land, but he flew a bit too close to the mouse's face.

The already frightened little mouse squealed, "Man! Get back, Jack! What do you want little, bee? I'll chew your face off too, man! Get away from me! Shoo!"

"Excuse me, little mouse. My name is Bubba... And I have a very bad cold," Bubba stopped to let out a weak cough. "And I was thinking since you're a little mouse and all, that you would know where I could find the Great White Owl..."

"Man! Oh, don't say that, man!" yelled El Chico. "Oh, El Great White Owl es muy no-no! No-no! You don't say that, man! Okay? You don't say that! You, Seńor Bubba Bee, why don't you go get some honey from a flower, man? And take it back to your la casa hive, huh? El Great White Owl, I'll chew his face off! You don't say that anymore, okay? Okay?" pleaded El Chico, who looked over his shoulder for an owl each time he said, "Okay?"

Something was telling Bubba that the little mouse was more than a little afraid of the Great White Owl. So, Bubba thought it best not to mention the Owl's proper name again.

"Okay, little mouse. I won't say that anymore. Anyway, I was hoping to find the... You-Know-Who, because Stinky Paws without the honey...You know, the fox who was going to have you for lunch? He told me about the... You-Know-Who. And he might have a cure for my cough so I don't have to go back to my bee-hive and get yelled at by my mama and get a stingin' from my papa and…"

"Sting?" interrupted El Chico. "Man! You sting me, I'll chew your face and your body, too! Oh you, Seńor Bubba Bee, you're starting to get on my nerves! Oooooo!" warned El Chico.

"Chew, chew, chew...Too many chews," thought Bubba. "Don't worry, little mouse. I won't sting you, little mouse. Do you know where in the forest the You-Know-Who lives? Huh, little mouse?"

At this point, being called "little mouse," along with Bubba's many questions, was upsetting enough to cause El Chico Mouse to feel like chewing on Bubba's face. But, with what little control he had left, the little mouse found himself answering Bubba's questions. And he didn't even know why.

"Señor Bubba Bee, don't call me 'little mouse,' okay? Okay? Me llamo El Chico Mouse. I will tell you where El You-Know-Who lives, Señor Bubba Bee. El Chico Mouse will tell you, a small, little, tiny, poquito Bubba Bee where El You-Know-Who lives. Okay? El You-Know-Who lives on top of a muy grande mountain en el cave in the middle a la forest, way, way over there," said El Chico, pointing toward a forest. "Go back to your la casa hive, Bubba Bee...A mountain with an owl on top of it is no place for you, Señor Bubba Bee. No matter how much mi mama and mi papa get mad with me, Bubba Bee...They always give me…cheese."

"I can't go back, El Chico Mouse...Not without a cure for my cold," replied Bubba.

"Escuchen, Bubba Bee...Es muy importante!" the mouse said. "El You-Know-Who will eat you up at night faster than you can say, 'habaneros con honey.' You won't go back to your la casa hive, Señor Bubba Bee? Okay, then El Chico Mouse is going to give you, the smallest Bubba Bee en el mundo, advice. Go see El You-Know-Who after he eats his dinner. If you see him before he eats his dinner... Que lastima! He'll eat...your face...OFF! Comprende, Bubba Bee?"

Bubba let out a weak cough and gulped, "Comprende! Thank-you, El Chico Mouse. Oh, and a...thank you for not chewing my face off, too!"

"Adios, amigo bee."

"Adios, El Chico Mouse."

Bubba flew away from El Chico Mouse in his search of El You-Know-Who through the deep, dark forest. He flew for the longest time, but there was no sign of a mountain. Bubba could only see the giant redwoods and the setting sun. As the sun was going down, Bubba's confidence was going down. Feeling like he was lost, he decided to fly closer to the ground to see about asking for more directions. And then, he saw a slow moving turtle heading toward a stream. Perhaps the turtle could help guide Bubba to the mountain of the Great White, um...El You-Know-Who.

This time Bubba landed very carefully and with near perfection right in front of the turtle. He was so proud of his smooth landing that he stood tall, let out a slight cough to clear his throat, and very politely introduced himself like a perfect gentleman...a gentle-bee.

"Hello, Mr. Turtle. My name's Bubba Bartholomew Buzzbee and I have a very unpleasant ailment for which I shall need to find a cure. I fear a cure shall be needed very soon or I shall face a rather unpleasant stinging from my father."

"A bee! Oh, oh!" yelled the turtle.

As soon as the turtle heard the word, "stinging" he quickly tucked all parts of his body into the safety of his shell.

"Hello, Mr. Turtle?' shouted Bubba as he knocked on the hard turtle shell.

"Don't worry! I'm not going to sting you! Please come out!" begged Bubba, as his knocking continued.

"Go away!" muttered the turtle, still inside his shell.

"Please, Mr. Turtle! I need to find the mountain where El You-Know-Who lives before it gets too dark," pleaded Bubba. "Don't worry, Mr. Turtle. I'm not going to sting you! Please...I can't go back to the hive now. I'm not allowed to fly at night."

When several moments had passed without a response from the turtle, Bubba began to cry. As Bubba continued crying, the turtle poked his head out of his shell and watched Bubba cry for as long as he could stand to watch a bee cry.

"Oh, quit your crying!" commanded the turtle. "Here! Blow your nose!"

The Turtle popped out of his shell holding a hand-kerchief toward Bubba's nose.

"Thank-you, Mr. Turtle. That's very kind of you," replied Bubba, as he politely rubbed his nose on what looked like the cleanest spot on the handkerchief.

"Quit calling me 'Mr. Turtle!' My name is Oscar. Now what is a 'You-Know-Who'?" Oscar firmly asked.

"A You-Know-Who, Oscar? El You-Know-Who isn't a 'what'," replied Bubba.

"Oh, bother! Will you please skip your busy-bee attitudes and speed it up a bit? I'm on a very rigid and demanding sleeping schedule!" complained Oscar.

Bubba then responded very rapidly to the sleepy and angered turtle in one single breath.

"Okay, Oscar. El You-Know-Who is the Great White Owl that Stinky Paws without the honey told me about before El Chico Mouse said the Great White Owl was a 'no-no'. And El Chico Mouse was going to chew my face off, so I had to call the Great White Owl El You-Know-Who. Now do you understand, Oscar?" exclaimed Bubba, letting out a cough and catching his breath at the same time.

Oscar looked at Bubba in utter confusion and said, "What?"

Bubba repeated himself in the same manner as be-
fore: "El You-Know-Who is the Great White Owl that
Stinky Paws without the honey told me about…before EI
Chico Mouse was going to chew my face off."

"Oh, never mind!" commanded Oscar. "Listen, bee! Why is a sniveling, snuffling, and possibly contagious germ-shuttle like you wanting to talk with the Great One, especially during his dinner break and my precious bedtime? Why don't you just fly home and call it a day?" asked Oscar.

"I can't go home, Oscar," replied Bubba, as he paused to let out a weak cough. "I just have to find a cure for my cough and cold. Besides, it's too late, and my mama and papa are already upset with me."

"At least you have parents...even if they are upset with you. Sometimes having angry parents is better than not having any at all. Bubba?" Oscar calmly asked.

"Yes, Oscar?"

"If I tell you the way to the Great One's mountain, will you promise to leave me alone so I can get my beauty sleep?"

"I promise, Oscar."

"Bubba?"

"Yes, Oscar?"

"Do you see the top of that mountain over there, just over those treetops?"

Bubba looked in disbelief and bellowed, "Do you mean the mountain was right over there and I didn't even see it? How could I have missed it, Oscar?"

"Maybe you have more than just a cough and a cold?" replied Oscar. "Or maybe you need some glasses... or a map? Or just maybe you would like me to blow on my horn and announce you to the Great One?" replied Oscar as he had pulled out each item mentioned from inside his shell.

"No, thank you, Oscar. I think I can find the mountain by myself."

As Oscar quickly tucked all parts of himself and his belongings back inside his shell he blurted out, "Well, then...Alrighty now...Good night, Bubba. Remember your promise!"

"Oh thank you, Oscar!" shouted Bubba, joyously knocking on Oscar's shell. "Good night, Oscar! Sleep tight!"

"Go away! You just broke your promise," muttered Oscar from inside the shell.

Well, Bubba was finally on his way to the mountain of the Great One. As you can well imagine, Bubba was feeling a bit nervous about meeting an owl at night, let alone a Great One. The sun was down and it was dark by the time Bubba reached the top of the Great White Owl's domain.

At last, Bubba saw the eerie opening of a dark cave. And as Bubba flew toward the opening, he wondered if the Great One had eaten his dinner yet. But as scared as he was, he landed right smack on the Great One's doorstep. With a cough and a lump in his throat, Bubba gasped, "Door-step? Huh?"

Then he called out, "Great One?" That didn't work. "You-who! El You-Know-Who?" That didn't work, either. "Great White Owl? Not working!"

After a long pause, a fierce sounding voice from inside the cave echoed, "Cut out that whoo nonsense! What do you want?"

"Excuse me, is that you? You know, Mr. El, One, Great White Who Owl? My name is Bubba... And I have a very bad cold and…"

"Go away, I'm not home!" shouted the voice inside the cave. The awesome sound of the voice echoing in the cave made Bubba feel like going back to his beehive only to receive a certain stingin'. But, it was so dark by now, he just couldn't give up and fly back to the hive. He'd rather face the Great White Owl than his own papa. "Mr. Great White Owl, I just have to talk with you!" yelled Bubba, boldly.

"I'm warning you! You had better leave. It's my dinner time!" echoed the voice again, this time even more fiercely. At this point, Bubba had a notion to try something he hadn't done since he got his left wing caught in a piece of string. Bubba took a moment to pray:

Dear Lord, I'm sorry
I didn't listen to mama.
Please help me find a cure
for my cold and don't let
me get eaten by Mr. Great
White Owl.

P.S. I'm scared.

Amen.

Just as Bubba finished his prayer he braved to enter the deep, dark cave, hopefully not as an appetizer for the owl. As Bubba flew inside the dark entrance, he couldn't see anything but a flickering light, dimly shimmering on a cave wall. And as Bubba flew toward the light, he could see what appeared to be the massive wingspan of the Great One, casting its gloomy shadow on the cave wall. Bubba tried not to show any fear and figured to be on his best, most polite beehavior.

"Mmm…Mr. Great White Owl, sir. Stinky Paws without the honey told me that you could help me find a cure for my cold. And El Chico Mouse told…"

"Stinky Paws? Without the honey?" shouted the Great One. "What kind of whoowee-poowee are you talking about? Wait a moment! I need my glasses... I can't see who I'm talking to."

The Great One fumbled around for his glasses, mumbling to himself in frustration at not being able to find them so quickly. "Ah, there! Now I can... Wait a second, here! You're a honey bee! What's a pesky little vermin doing in my cave?" asked the owl in disbelief.

"Mr. Great White Owl...Mr. Great One, sir? I sure hope you're not thinking of eating something somewhere else in this room. Like maybe a..." Bubba let out another cough with a brief sniffle of his nose. "Like maybe you're not thinking about eating a pesky little sick vermin, Mr. Great White Owl?"

"Well if this ain't like getting muddy water on your tail feathers!" said the slightly confused owl, then letting out a cough. "You know something there, Bumba?"

"It's Bubba."

"Whooever!" the owl said, coughing again. "My wife Owlivia once told me, 'Owly, never bug a bee 'cause they'll sting ya for no reason, no matter what the season.' She never told me what to do when a bee bugs you, though. Nope! She never said anything about that. But, I think I know what to do with a little coughing honey bee...yep," said the owl with another cough.

"Ya know, here I am suffering with this nasty cough, and here your are a sick little honey bee named Bubba, buzzing around in my cave asking me about my dinner that I didn't even have a chance to finish!" complained the owl, but mostly to himself.

"Mr. Great White Owl?"

"What?"

"Do you mean you have a cold, too?" asked Bubba, amazed that he had something in common with the Great One.

"Jumpin' Jack rabbits! What do you think I've been doing the last few moments? I haven't exactly been coughing up fur balls, you know! Of course I have a cold!" exclaimed the Great White Owl. "I was out hunting late last night. I figured it was too cold, but I up and went anyway. Now, suppose you tell me about this Stinky Paws who lost his honey and what he told you about me!"

"Mr. Great White Owl, I came to see you because Stinky Paws without the honey told me about you. He told me that you could help me find a cure for my cold before El Chico Mouse told me that you were a no-no before your dinner break. And then Oscar...He's a turtle, and…"

"Wait just a minute there, Bubba! I'm starting to get all twisted up here, or maybe you're all twisted up, one of the two. Speaking of dinner breaks, I can't think too straight without some more food in my stomach," said the Great White Owl with another cough. "Especially with this nasty cough."

At this point, The Great One ever so slowly blinked his right eye and studied the sickly, tired-looking bee. Then, with almost a kind heart he uttered, "Now, I suppose since you've come all the way up this here mountain with a cold, you might as well stay and help me finish my dinner. Ain't no sense in kicking you out into the coldness of the night as long as you don't figure on stinging me. Because if you even think about stinging me, I'll have you for dessert! So let's eat."

Getting invited by an owl to eat "owl food" was not what Bubba wanted to hear. Once again, Bubba had to choose his next words carefully, so as not to insult the Great One's kind offer.

"I wouldn't think of stinging you, Mr. Great White Owl, but I can't, I mean I...Is your dinner still alive?" asked Bubba, who had heard what owls normally eat from his papa.

"Is my dinner still alive?" The Great White Owl began to laugh and cough, uncontrollably wheezing out, "Of course not!"

"And you want me to eat 'it' with you?" asked Bubba, who was disturbed by the thought of what "it" might be.

"Of course I do! Now you're the one who came all the way up here invading my cave looking for a cure for your cold, asking me a bunch of silly questions, and telling me about a Stinky fella who ran out of honey and a mouse who says I'm a 'no-no.' Do you want to get rid of that blasted cold, or don't you?"

"Of course I do, Mr. Great White Owl. I was really hoping you were going to cure my cold. But, if you're just going to sit there and laugh at me and make me eat that...that disgusting whatever it is or whoever it was... then you're nothing but a plain-old, ordinary, everyday, nobody owl! I'm not going to eat it! So, I might as well just go back to my beehive and face my papa!" exclaimed Bubba.

"Hold on there, Bubba! I don't think you know who you're talking to or what you're talking about! I don't know what you think is so disgusting about eating honey. But, if you're any kind of a honey bee, with or without a cold, you had better get used to it!"

"Honey?" said Bubba, in disbelief. "Mr. Great White Owl, do you mean you ate honey for dinner?"

"Had to!" confirmed the Great White Owl. "I don't know of a better cure for a cold. You should know that, Bubba. After all, don't you honey bees make the stuff? Yep, honey... best thing for a cold. You didn't have to come all this way to find that out. Anybody could have told you that... even a 'nobody' owl," said the owl, almost to himself.

Just then, Bubba remembered the words of his mama:

"You've got to eat your honey, honey, or you're gonna catch a cold."

"Mr. Great White Owl, I'm sorry I called you 'nobody' owl. I think I want to stay for dinner, if you still want me to eat it with you."

"Now that's the most sensible thing you've said since you got here. Incidentally, there Bubba, I told you how I got my cold. How'd you catch yours?" asked the Great White Owl.

"It's a long story, Mr. Great White Owl."

"Well, why don't we fetch us some honey and sit down and talk about it there, Bubba?"

"Okay, Mr. Great White Owl…I think I'm ready for some honey now…I think I'm ready for some honey now. I think I'm ready for some honey…"

As Bubba repeated himself, he was slowly awakening from a dream. With his head on his desk and his mama standing near him, he again said, "I think I'm ready for some honey..."

Bubba stopped there and was now awake.

"Alright, baby. Wake up," said Bubba's mama.

"Mama! I was just talking to the Great White Owl! I mean...I flew away from the hive and talked to Stinky Paws without the honey...and El Chico Mouse... and then, a very sleepy turtle named, Oscar."

"Sure you did, Bubba ... sure you did," said Bubba's mama, not believing a single word Bubba was saying. "And now you're ready for some honey?"

"Yes mama...of course! Even the Great White Owl eats honey."

"Bubba, dear. I'm so sorry I yelled at you the way I did."

"It's okay, mama. I was wrong, too. But mama, I was talking to the Great White Owl!"

Just then, Bubba's papa entered his bedroom and said, "What's this I hear about a Great White Owl?"

"Papa! I talked to the Great White Owl! He was huge and he wears glasses. And Oscar, he's a turtle...he was mean at first, but he's not really that mean at all..."

"Alright Bubba, slow down. I can't wait to hear all about your adventure. But just let me check in with mom first to see how your day went," said his papa.

"Bubba was just fine, dear. He did just fine. Bubba? Go ahead and tell papa about your adventure."

"Thanks, mama. Papa! There was this little mouse; his name was El Chico. And he almost got eaten by a fox. His name was Stinky paws. And Oscar, he's a turtle, and he pulled out a map and horn..."

Well, Bubba was only dreaming, of course. And, through his dream he finally realized that the cure for his cold was right inside the beehive the whole time. However, through the Great White Owl Bubba learned no matter how old or how young or whoo you are, "You've got to eat your honey, honey."

And so ends the story of Bubba the Coughing Bee, otherwise known as the bee who had a very bad cold.

the
end

CPSIA information can be obtained
at www.ICGtesting.com
Printed in the USA
JSHW030255170421
13658JS00005B/97